LITTLE LION

Inspiring | Educating | Creating | Entertaining

Brimming with creative inspiration, how-to projects, and useful information to enrich your everyday life, quarto.com is a favorite destination for those pursuing their interests and passions.

First published in 2022 by QEB Publishing,
an imprint of The Quarto Group.
100 Cummings Center,
Suite 265D Beverly,
MA 01915, USA.
T (978) 282-9590 F (978) 283-2742
www.quarto.com

Editorial Assistant: Alice Hobbs
Art Director: Susi Martin
Publisher: Holly Willsher

A CIP record for this book is available from the Library of Congress.

ISBN: 978-0-7112-7409-9

9 8 7 6 5 4 3 2 1

Manufactured in Guangdong, China TT032022

MIX
Paper from responsible sources
FSC® C016973

LITTLE LION

ANNA BRETT

illustrated by
CARMEN SALDAÑA

Good morning, I'm Little Lion!

I've just woken up as the warm sun
is rising over the grasslands
of the African savanna.

Spend the day with me
and let me introduce you to my family
and our home.

My mom goes out hunting most
nights so we can start the day
with a big breakfast.

I drank her milk for the first
few months of my life,
but I'm starting to really enjoy
the taste of meat now.

I live with my mom, my siblings,
lots of aunts and cousins, and my dad.
Our group is called a pride.

Dad has the most amazing fluffy
mane of hair around his head.
My brothers will all grow one
as they get older.

I have got spots on my fur,
but Mom says they'll fade and I'll look
like her in another couple of years.

Mom is having a snooze which means
playtime for me and my siblings.

We love roughhousing with each other.
I'm practicing my leaping so I'll be ready to go
out hunting one day.

All that running around has made me thirsty, so it's time to head down to the water hole for a drink and a bath.

In the dry season, when the water hole disappears, we have to suck the liquid out of plants instead.

My mom is the best! She takes care of me
and teaches me the skills to survive.

She also loves my cousins and we
are all one big family.

If I'm a little tired, she'll pick me up by
the scruff of my neck and carry me along.

My dad is the biggest lion you've ever seen.
His mane is long, his teeth are huge,
and his claws are sharp.

His role is to protect the pride from danger.
He has got a few scars from the battles he's
fought, but he knows to be gentle with us.

This afternoon my aunt is introducing
her cubs to the pride for the first time.
It's so exciting!

She's been hidden away in a den for the past
six weeks to give birth and help the cubs
learn to walk.

She has to remind Dad, and me,
to be gentle with the babies.

I spy my older brother.
He's about to leave our pride to try and
form his own. Dad gives a loud roar
to remind him that he's old enough to
survive on his own now.

Other males often try and take over our
pride, but Dad fights them off.

Uh-oh, Dad's roaring again,
and this time it means danger.

Some hyenas are trying to grab our leftovers from breakfast. The adults spring into action as we are told to stay out of the way.

23

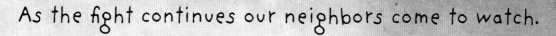

As the fight continues our neighbors come to watch.

We share our land with many different animals,
but Dad marks out our territory using his urine
as a scent to create a border that they,
and other prides of lions, know not to cross.

25

Although our neighbors and the hyenas
are no match for Mom and Dad, they are a lot
bigger than us cubs and Mom has told us
to stay away from them.

She's taught us how to climb trees and use
our claws so we can stay safe.

Mom roars to tell us it's now safe to come down from the tree, since the hyenas have gone.

Dad has kept us all safe once again. But the adults have a few cuts and bruises to tend to. We all come together to rest and take care of each other.

A storm is brewing tonight, but it doesn't worry us. In fact, it makes it easier to hunt because the noise and wind keep Mom and the other lionesses hidden from prey like wildebeest.

My aunts are speedy and chase the prey toward
Mom in the hope that one becomes isolated.
She can then pounce and use all her strength to
overpower it.

I'm sleepy!

It's been a busy day for the whole pride
as Mom has provided us with food, Dad has
kept us safe, and the other cubs and I have had a
great time climbing and playing.

I love my family and can't wait to see
what adventures we'll have tomorrow.

Goodnight, everyone!

FUN FACTS

I hope you enjoyed spending time with me and my family. Would you like to learn more about us? Let me tell you everything!

- Lions are the only cats that live in groups.

- The group is called a pride and can include up to 20 individuals.

A lion's roar can be heard up to 5 miles away.

- Babies are called cubs and they have light spots on their fur when they are born to help camouflage them.

- Lions spend 16 hours or more per day resting and sleeping.

- A female lion is called a lioness.

FACT FILE

Body length: Males average 6.5 feet, females average 5 feet

Tail length: 3 feet

Weight:
Males average 420 pounds, females average 290 pounds

Speed: Up to 50 miles per hour

MANES AND PAWS

A lion's foot is called a paw. They have five toes on the front paws and four toes on the back paws, all with sharp claws at the end. Can you spot the odd paw print in this trail?

Only male lions have a mane. It starts to grow from around the age of two. Which shadow matches this magnificent male lion?

RRRRRROOOAR

a

b

c

d

HELPING HANDS

Sadly, lions are classed as a vulnerable species of animal. This means they are at risk of becoming extinct in the wild. Extinct means there are no individuals left alive anymore.

African lion cub in the wild.

The Gir National Park in India runs a special breeding programme to help boost lion numbers.

Conservation is the way that humans can help keep endangered animals safe. Lions are threatened by habitat loss and hunting, so conservation focuses on educating people about not destroying their grassland habitats and making the hunting of lions illegal.

Currently, there are around 20,000 lions living in Africa, but just 600 in India. Lions used to be found in great numbers all across Africa and Asia.

Male Asiatic lions are a little smaller than their African cousins.

Male and female African lions on the savanna.

Asiatic lions can be found in the Gir National Park in the north of India.

FAMILY AND FRIENDS

Lionesses usually give birth to between one and five cubs at a time. Count how many cute cubs you can see in this scene.

Can you choose the correct jigsaw piece to complete this picture of the animals that share the savanna with lions?

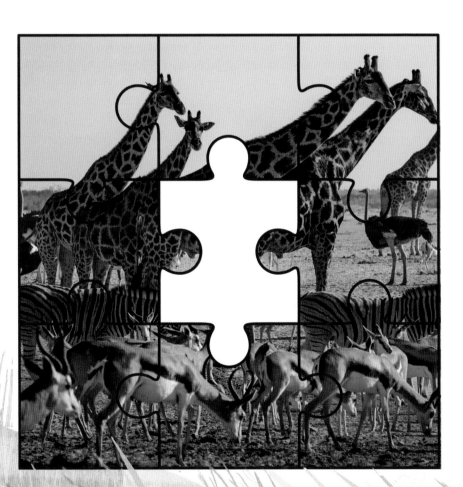

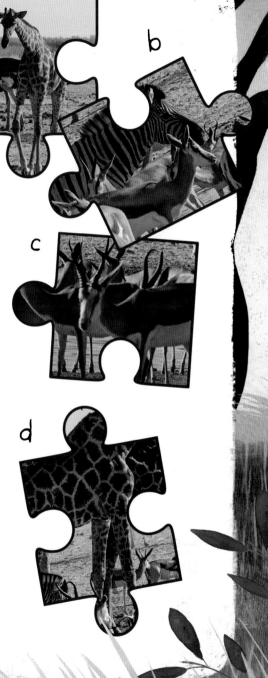

a

b

c

d

FRILLY FACE ART

Make a paper plate lion face with a frilly mane.

YOU WILL NEED

- A white paper plate
- Yellow, gold, and orange paper (color in your own if you don't have any!)
- Yellow, orange, and black coloring pencils, pens, crayons, or paint
- String
- Scissors
- Glue

1 Start your project by coloring in your paper plate. You want to use orange around the edge and yellow in the middle. See if you can blend the colors a little where they meet.

2 Ask an adult to help you cut your yellow, gold, and orange paper into long strips, about half an inch thick. Wrap a strip of paper around a pencil to create a tight coil and then pull the pencil out.

3 Unroll about an inch of your coil and glue it to the edge of your plate. Continue to do this with more strips of paper, sticking them all the way around the plate, but leave a gap between each one. You can use whatever color you want!

4 Repeat step 3, but this time stick your strips a little closer to the center of the plate and in the gaps you left in step 3. Finally, fill in any gaps with extra strips of gold coiled paper to create the most amazing mane.

5 It's time to draw on your lion's face with your black pen. Add two big eyes, a triangle-shaped nose, and a lovely smile below it.

6 Finally, cut six pieces of string, 1.5–2 inches in length. Glue three whiskers onto each side of your lion's nose. Now enjoy showing off your *raw-some* lion!

WHITE LIONS

Very occasionally African lions are born with white fur. It doesn't cause any problems for the lion, but their beauty makes them very interesting to humans!

These special lions have fur that ranges from blonde to almost completely white. It's very different to the usual tawny color of lions.

Males have white manes and tail tips as well.

Most white lions are found in zoos or wildlife centers. But the wild Birmingham pride in the Ngala Private Game Reserve in Africa is very special because it has two white lions.

When white lions are found in the wild they are regarded as sacred by some African cultures. It's thought they originate from the Timbavati region of South Africa.

QUIZ

Test your knowledge about lions with this fun quiz. Can you score ten out of ten?

1. Do male or female lions have a mane?

2. What is a group of lions called?

3. Which of these noises does a lion not make: roar, meow, tweet, grunt?

4. True or false: lions eat meat.

5. Lion cubs look a little different than their parents because they have what on their fur?

6. True or false: it never rains on the savannah where African lions live.

7. What do cubs drink when they are babies?

8. Which of these can lions do: climb trees or burrow underground?

9. True or false: only male lions go out hunting.

10. Which of these do lions most like to hunt as prey: mammals, birds, or fish?

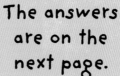

The answers are on the next page.

ANSWERS

P 36-37

P 40-41

Five cubs

Quiz answers

1. Male lions
2. A pride
3. Lions don't tweet!
4. True
5. Spots
6. False: it rains for half of the year
7. Milk
8. They can climb trees
9. False: female lions do most of the hunting
10. Lions mostly hunt mammals such as wildebeest